GOODBYE FEAR

Sandra F. Holt

www.TrueVinePublishing.org

Goodbye Fear
Sandra F. Holt

Published by
True Vine Publishing Co.
P.O. Box 22448
Nashville, TN 37202
www.TrueVinePublishing.org

ISBN: 978-1-956469-21-9 Paperback
ISBN: 978-1-956469-22-6 eBook

Printed in the United States—First Print

DEDICATION

My family and close friends, who listened to several drafts of this book as I wrote from my heart as God spoke to me. You are all such a blessing in my life. I also dedicate this book to my many readers and I am speaking prophetically. To you I am an unknown author, but a known author to God as He inspired me to write. I encourage you to read this book. It is filled with God's Word. There are valuable truths in this book that proclaim God's promises and deliverances. Since completing the first draft of this book, I cease not to pray for those of you who will pick up this book and won't be able to put it down until you come to know that fear can be part of your past, but absent from your present and future in Jesus' Name. I pray you all will say: Goodbye Fear.

TABLE OF CONTENTS

PREFACE

This Spiritual Book is composed of three major points: What is Fear? What is the Root of Fear? How to Get Rid of Fear? It is designed to provide you wisdom keys to address any kind of fear you may be dealing with in your life. God does not want us to live in fear, and that is why I felt compelled to write this book. It is time we stop letting Satan's lies and deceptions cause us to fear. Let's take authority over fear today in Jesus' name. This book contains my own personal testimonies that I pray will inspire you to take your proper position, using the Word of God to bring healing and deliverance in all areas of your life.

INTRODUCTION: GOODBYE FEAR

Do you live in fear? Does it rule your life or keep you from stepping out to perform your dreams? Do you worry about the unknown? Are you terrified at the possibility of being alone? Do sickness and disease frighten you? Do you worry about failing? If you answer yes to any of these questions or similar ones, it's time to acknowledge your fear and let it go! I assure you it will not let you go and it will try to torment you for the rest of your life if you allow it. Do you want to be tormented for the rest of your life? I know you do not. Maybe you, like millions of others, have been battling with fear for a long time, but it's time to be set free. Jesus said that He came to heal the broken-hearted and set the captives free. Let Jesus set you free today!

Currently there is a lot of fear evident in the world. This pandemic has shown us that many are battling with anxiety every day. Some people are losing hope, not knowing what to do. Distress has gripped so many who are wondering if this pandemic will ever end. Although it seems as if things are getting better, some are still wondering if this is truly the end of this pandemic. Many desire for their lives to go back to normal. There have also been worries regarding the benefits of taking the vaccine versus not taking the vaccine, not to mention the fear that has been evident due to the huge loss of lives. When it comes to the vaccine, I am not taking sides either way, but I see how fear has reared its ugly head even among the body of Christ in addition to the world.

I pray that if you are dealing with this, that you take a stand and say no more. I look at fear as being a pandemic itself that needs to end, as it was never meant to rule our lives. We have to stop allowing it. The truth of the matter is that it can only have the power we give it. I encourage you to take your power back; take your peace back in Jesus' Name.

Proverbs 28:1 says, "The wicked flee when no man pursueth: but the righteous are bold as a lion".

God has called us to be bold as a lion. When we are bold as a lion, then we become fearless. Fear cannot rule over the righteous. God has told us how we should see ourselves and how we should be. He compares us to a lion. The lion is king of the jungle. Although a lion is not the largest animal in the jungle, he sees himself as powerful and fearless. That is how we should be. God wants us to have the boldness to believe it and to see ourselves like a lion sees himself. Let it be understood, we are kings of our destiny with the strength of the Lord, and fear should not have any part of our lives.

I wrote this book because I know all too well how fear will try to torment you. I am currently 57 years old as I write this book. My age will become a little more significant towards the end of this book. I believe this book has been anointed by God to assist you in being set free from fear. In this book, I will share some of my own personal experiences, revealing how fear started in my life and how God delivered and set me free.

I truly pray that God will use this book to deliver you from fear. Satan came to steal, kill and destroy, and fear is a component to assist him in doing the job. I pray through the Holy Spirit that after reading this book, you will take your proper place as a child of God and proclaim with assurance "No More Fear!"

2 Timothy 1:7 says, "For God hath not given us the spirit of fear; but of power, and of love, and of a sound mind."

That is a powerful scripture. Look at what God has given us. Why are we not using the spirit of power, love, and a sound mind? That's what God wants for us. It is time we take what God has given us and reject what Satan wants to place on us. Satan has tormented you long enough. Hasn't he? God wants you to live a life of peace and not a life of torment. God does not want us ignorant of Satan's devices, so fear has to go in Jesus' Name!

WHAT IS FEAR?

I heard it defined that fear is false evidence appearing real, and I think that is an understandable concept. It has a nice cliché to it. But personally, I see it as an evil spiritual force from Satan aimed at destroying you, your family, and your dreams. The truth is that no one wants to live in fear, but many of us do every day. We fear things will not work out. We fear disease. We fear what tomorrow holds. We fear God will not answer our prayers.

Fear, Fear, Fear... This becomes debilitating and tormenting. We give fear so much power. Why is that? Let's change that course today. What if we give faith in God as much power as we give fear from Satan? Where would we be? Satan wants to rob us of our faith and fill our hearts with fear. He knows that when faith in God takes its proper seat, fear loses its grip on our life.

> **"FEAR FROM SATAN IS AN EVIL SPIRIT THAT WANTS TO KEEP YOU IN BONDAGE"**

Many of us associate fear with an emotion. No - it is much more than just an emotion. Fear from Satan is an evil spirit that wants to keep you in bondage, because fear is bondage. You have to stand your ground against your own emotions if you are to gain a victory over fear. I know you want that victory. No one wants to live in fear, but many fall into that demonic trap every day. You may say, "But you don't understand, I feel fear." I repeat, it is so much more than a feeling or an emotion. Know this - it is an avenue that Satan uses to gain access over us to cause havoc in our lives. You may ask, "How does he gain access?" Satan gains access through your mind. The mind is powerful, and if he can get you to meditate and worry, you have just given him access. I encourage you to speak the Word of God over that situation and over your life. You may have to just shut your mind off. Say to your mind: "Me and God are working on something." Talk to that fear and say: "You will no longer control and torment me. I will live the peaceful life God wants me to live and I will not live in fear!"

In fact, God wants us to stand our ground and refuse to fear. It is also important that we watch the words we say. Many times, we say things contrary to God's Word because of fear. Don't let fear cause you to say something opposite of God's Word. If we ever understand the revelation of the power of our words, how spiritually liberating that will be! You may be a little cynical and say, "How can words change my situation?" Let me ask you a question. If fear is tormenting your life, what do you have to lose? Why wouldn't you be open to God's Word bringing healing and deliverance to you? Declare God's promises over your life today. How do you declare God's promises? With God's Word. Satan is waiting for you to speak fear so he can make it a reality. Don't let Him. God wants you to speak faith in Him so He can make His promises through your faith a reality.

"DECLARE GOD'S PROMISES OVER YOUR LIFE TODAY."

God is immeasurably more powerful than Satan, and God is able to cause us to triumph every time we put our trust in Him. See, we must operate in faith. How does one get to faith? Romans 10:17 says, "Faith cometh by hearing, and hearing by the Word of God." The Word of God builds our faith when we take His Word and apply it over every circumstance in our lives. Hear God's Word today!

Job 3:25 says, "For the thing which I greatly feared is come upon me, and that which I was afraid of is come unto me."

We find Job continuously offering sacrifices to God in case his sons had sinned and cursed

God in their hearts. He worried continuously about his family. Maybe that's where you are. You worry about your children, grandchildren, parents or another family member or friend. Job did not have to worry and live in fear, and neither do you. Job could have expressed his concerns to God and spoken his children's deliverance. I do believe Job finally came to the point and realized that, but it was not before hardship and pain. Oh, what needless pain we bear all because we do not take our burdens to the Lord in prayer. Can I get an Amen? Take that fear to God and expect deliverance. Say: "I am fear-free and I refuse to live in fear". Make that declaration and hold unto it. God will strengthen you.

Maybe some of you have children who appear to be living contrary to the Word of God, as Job's possibly were. I encourage you to speak God's Word over their lives. Decree scriptures like Psalm 91, which provides protection and the assurance for those who abide under the shadow of the Almighty. There is peace and safety in God.

My daughter and son-in-law are both schoolteachers. Due to the initial unknowns about the coronavirus I went to my daughter's classroom to speak Psalm 91, knowing she had concerns.

We declared the promises and protection of God over her and her classroom. I encourage that scripture when praying for protection for you and your family. I decreed Psalms 91 and God protected her. I encouraged my son-in-law to stand on that scripture as well and God protected him too.

See, I have come to understand that there is power in our words, and when we decree God's promises, He will fulfill them. Imagine that the curtains were pulled back, figuratively speaking, and God showed you all that was accomplished through your words good or bad. What would that look like? What would you see? Would you want to recant many of those words spoken that did not agree with God's Word? I believe you would. Many of us would. You may not be able to take past spoken words back, but you can have a fresh start from this moment by declaring what God says. Again, words are so powerful.

Philippians 4: 6-7 says, "Be careful for nothing; but in everything by prayer and supplication with thanksgiving let your requests be

> **"IMAGINE...GOD SHOWED YOU ALL THAT WAS ACCOMPLISHED THROUGH YOUR WORDS GOOD OR BAD. WHAT WOULD THAT LOOK LIKE?:"**

made known unto God. And the peace of God, which passeth all understanding, shall keep your hearts and minds through Christ Jesus." God is telling us: Don't worry! God has given us His Word to focus on. Commit everything to him in prayer. We have to believe God's Word as they are truth and life. God's Word brings peace. Through this pandemic, many have lacked peace. As the body of Christ, we should point the world to the peace of God but we too are suffering due to fear. Peace only comes from God. In His arms are safety and protection. It's time to rest. Haven't you lived in torment long enough? Know your authority. Make your request known to God.

Let us get to the point that we lay our concerns, our worry, our anxiety and our fears on God. Matthew 11:28-29 says, "Come unto me, all ye that labour and are heavy laden, and I will give you rest. Take my yoke upon you and learn of me; for I am meek and lowly in heart: and ye shall find rest unto your souls." Again, Jesus said, "Come unto me all that labor and are heavy laden and I will give you rest." He is not talking about when we get to Heaven. We are not going to be heavily laden in Heaven. There are no burdens in Heaven, no demonic forces, no evil, no fear. He is talking about NOW! He goes on to say, "My yoke is easy and my burdens are light." Fear should be laid on Jesus and He never meant for us to live in fear. Why would Jesus go to the cross, and shed his blood so we could live in fear? It doesn't make sense and it should not. Declare today: "No More Fear!"

INFLUENCE OF THE MIND

1 Peter 5:8 (NIV), "Be alert and of sober mind. Your enemy the devil prowls around like a roaring lion looking for someone to devour."

Baker's Bible Dictionary defines the mind as the part of the human being in which thoughts take place, as well as perceptions and decisions to do good or evil. Every decision goes through the mind. Think about your everyday thought life. Everything you do is through your mind, which starts with a thought. You decide whether you will work, play, what to eat, what to wear, where to go and who to visit, etc. Have you noticed that even circumstances like the weather can influence your mind or mindset? For example, I know that sunny weather sometimes put me in a happier mindset then rainy weather.

The mind is so powerful. It is the essential component to function here on earth. Do you see why Satan wants to gain access to peoples' minds? Gaining access to our minds or thought life is the avenue that he is looking for to do his destructive evil work. Many of us have probably heard the statement, "An idle mind is the devil's workshop." Another word for idle is lazy.

This statement is not just talking about being slothful, but the influence Satan can have over an idle or lazy mind. We must know that he is the culprit of all the evil that is going on in the world and he is looking for men and women that he can influence. That influence begins with the mind. What happens when Satan gains influence over someone's mind? Evil things happen when his corrupt way of thinking is acted upon. He wants to load people's minds with evil thoughts and deceive them to act on those evil thoughts. This is his tool to lure people in the wrong direction. If we are perfectly honest, evil thoughts enter everyone's mind, spiritual or unspiritual, but every individual has a choice as to whether they will act on those evil thoughts.

"FEAR IS AN EVIL THOUGHT FROM SATAN"

Can I share something with you? Fear is an evil thought from Satan. We should know that one of Satan's ultimate jobs is to try to get us to doubt what God says about us or what God wants for us. If he can get us to doubt God, then it opens the door to fear. God wants us to walk by faith, not by fear. God does not want fear from Satan to dominate our minds. That is why the Word of God says, "Casting down imaginations, and every high thing that exalteth itself against the knowledge of God and bringing into captivity every thought to the obedience of Christ" (2 Corinthians 10:5).

So, if your thoughts are contrary to what the Word of God says, then your thoughts are not of God but they are Satan's thoughts. God wants us to refuse to entertain any thought that is not of Him. Don't focus on them. Those thoughts have to be rejected. Why? Because if we entertain wrong thoughts and allow our minds to be poisoned, we are walking into Satan's trap. We can't ponder over them; we can't allow them to

> "...RECEIVE THE IMAGE GOD HAS FOR YOU AND REJECT THE IMAGE SATAN DESIRES FOR YOU"

manifest; we can't allow them to pollute us. I encourage you to receive the image God has for you and reject the image Satan desires for you.

John 8:44 lets us know that Satan is the father of lies. He is the father of lies because he is the originator of lying. You may ask, "How is this significant and how does it affect me?" You see, Satan's deception started in the garden of Eden. He lied and twisted God's Word, which led to the fall of all mankind. After planting seeds of doubt in Eve's mind with a question, he contradicted God's Word.

Proverbs 6 tells us that there are seven things that God hates, one being a lying tongue. Ephesians 4:27 says, "Neither give place to the devil". What does that mean? It means that Satan is looking for access, an entry way into your life. Again, how does he gain access? Through your mind, and God is saying to not permit him.

2 Corinthians 11:3 (Amplified) says, "But I am afraid that, even as the serpent beguiled Eve by his cunning, your minds may be corrupted *and* led away from the simplicity of [your sincere and] pure devotion to Christ". Here, Paul is speaking to the Church of Corinth of his concern that the church would be drawn away from God. Satan wanted to corrupt the minds of the people of Corinth. Why? To lure them away from God, as Paul stated. He is still using those same deceptive tactics today trying to draw people away from God.

Have you ever wondered how Satan was able to lure Eve into that trap to disobey God? He used the power of suggestion. Let's look at this occurrence in more depth. In Genesis 3: 3-5 ESV: "Now the serpent was more crafty than any other beast of the field that the LORD God had made. He said to the woman, "Did God actually say, 'You shall not eat of any tree in the garden'?" And the woman said to the serpent, "We may eat of the fruit of the trees in the garden, but God said, 'You shall not eat of the fruit of the tree that is in the midst of the garden, neither shall you touch it, lest you die.'" But the serpent said to the woman, "You will not surely die. For God knows that when you eat of it your eyes will be opened, and you will be like God, knowing good and evil." Look at what transpired. See how he lured Eve into the trap of entertaining what he said. How did she entertain that thought? Through the mind. The scripture says that when she saw that the tree was good for food, pleasant to the eyes, a tree that would make one wise, she took of the fruit and did eat and then gave to her husband with her and he did eat. Let's ponder over this for a moment. Instead of obeying God, Adam and Eve became disobedient to God's commands. Adam and Eve had access to everything they needed in garden. Now all of a sudden, they wanted access to this one tree God had told them not to eat of. What happened here? Eve engaged in a conversation with Satan. Satan's goal was to corrupt Eve's way of thinking and, unfortunately, he succeeded. From that moment of entertaining what Satan said, Eve opened the door to rebellion to God.

You see how, if we entertain the lies of Satan, what happens? It appears that instead of trusting God, Eve was now acting as if God was holding something back from her. We must know that God wants to protect us. That is why it is crucial to have the mind of Christ. Do you have understanding now? When did Eve start desiring the fruit? When Satan suggested it. Have you ever been about your day and, all of a sudden, the wrong thought entered your mind? Rest assured that was from Satan. It is time we cast those vain imaginations down. Again, we cannot control bad thoughts that enter into our minds, but we can control whether we act on them. Acting on bad thoughts is disobedience to God.

"SIN WILL TAKE YOU FARTHER THAN YOU WANT TO GO, KEEP YOU LONGER THAN YOU WANT TO STAY, AND COST YOU MORE THAN YOU ARE ABLE TO PAY."

I heard the saying, "Sin will take you farther than you want to go, keep you longer than you want to stay, and cost you more than you are able to pay". There's truth to that. When people act upon evil thoughts, that sin tempts people into Satan's deceptive trap of destruction. When Adam and Eve disobeyed God, then sin entered into the world and separated them spiritually from God. As a result, all mankind became spiritually separated from God.

Romans 5:12 says, "Wherefore, as by one man sin entered into the world, and death by sin; and so death passed upon all men, for that all have sinned." Romans 5:19 tells us, "For as by one man's disobedience many were made sinners, so by the obedience of one shall many be made righteous." Thank God for Jesus who reunited us back to God!

Did you know also that your mind is also full of unlimited potential? That's creativity. Genesis chapter 11 talks about how the whole earth was one language and speech. The people decided that they would build a tower to reach heaven. As a result, the Lord came down to see the city and tower, and the Lord said in Genesis 11: 6, "...Behold, the people is one, and they have all one language, and this they begin to do: and now nothing will be restrained from them, which they have imagined to do." That's potential. This is what can be accomplished when people put their minds together. God understood this because God created our imagination, but Satan understood this too. You see how dangerous it is when Satan tries to tap into the minds of people with unlimited potential who do not acknowledge God?

Philippians 2:5 says, "Let this mind be in you, which was also in Christ Jesus:"

God is calling us to have the mind of Christ. Why? Because Satan's agenda cannot accomplish anything with a believer who thinks like Jesus. Having the mind of Christ is prevailing. With this mind we follow Romans 12:2, which says in part, "And be not conformed to this world: but be ye transformed by the renewing of your mind...". To be transformed is to be changed. A changed mindset leads to spiritual maturity. With spiritually maturity, we are able to discern what the perfect will of God is.

Joyce Meyer said, "You cannot have a positive life and negative mind." That's powerful. If your life is to be positive than you need to get rid of a negative mindset, meaning cast down Satan's thoughts. I read a story about Stamatis Moraitis. He was a Greek war veteran that moved to the United States until he was diagnosed with terminal lung cancer. Nine doctors confirmed his diagnosis and he was told he had 9 months to live. He was offered aggressive treatment, but doctors told him that this treatment still would not save his life. He declined the treatment and he and his wife moved back to his native home, Ikaria. When he first moved back, he spent his days in bed. However, subsequently, he reconnected with his faith. He started hanging out with his friends and declared one day, "I might as well die happy". As the days went by, he started feeling better. Days turned into months. He lived past the nine months. He lived for many more years. Later he went back to the United States to ask his doctors about this experience but they had all died. He lived to be 102 (Lissa Rankin, November 27, 2013).

Although possibly his diet helped save his life, I believe that decision to die happy was perhaps a turning point. Again, this shows the power of the mind. What if he had just stayed in bed as he initially started doing? He probably would have died, but he refused to allow the thoughts of worrying over death control him. In essence, he was not afraid. He lived each day as if it was his last. If he was to have a positive life, he could not entertain negative thoughts. I encourage you to apply Philippians 4:8 to your life in which God provides us specifics things to focus our minds on.

Lamentations 3:21 says, "This I recall to my mind, therefore, have I hope." Here Jeremiah focused his mind on God in the most difficult circumstances. Regardless of how bad things may seem at times, with God on our side there is always hope. God is calling us to keep our minds on Him. The devil has no power over a person whose mind is focused on God.

Romans 7 tells us to serve the Law of God with our mind. With the mind of God, we allow him to think through us. We receive what God says about us. There are no limitations for God. God wants us to see ourselves free. He wants us to have a free mind trusting in Him and Him alone. He wants us to **"THERE ARE NO LIMITATIONS FOR GOD"** close the door to Satan's craftiness. Make the decision, "I will have the mind of Christ." That's what I constantly strive to do. That's what I pray for you as well. I encourage you from this day forward to not allow your mind to entertain Satan's evil thoughts no, let the mind of Christ dwell in you.

THE POWER OF OUR WORDS

Mathew 15:11 says, "Not that which goeth into the mouth defileth a man; but that which cometh out of the mouth, this defileth a man".

When I was a little girl, I remember hearing and saying these words, "Sticks and stones may break my bones, but words will never hurt me." Maybe as a child that phrase may have made some sense to me. But as an adult, I know that phrase is so far from the truth, as words are powerful and words do and can hurt. The truth of the matter is that words can build you up or tear you down. What do you think Satan wants to do with words? I believe you've guessed it. He wants to tear us down. He tries to accomplish this by getting others to speak negative words in our lives. Ephesians 4:29 (AMP) says, "Do not let unwholesome [foul, profane, worthless, vulgar] words ever come out of your mouth, but only such speech as is good for building up others, according to the need and the occasion, so that it will be a blessing to those who hear [you speak]". God tells us how he wants us to use words, how not to use words, and the purpose of words. In essence, He wants our words to be a blessing to build others up.

I think about my two little grandchildren. They love for me to affirm them and tell them how proud I am of them. In fact, if I tell one that I am proud and the other one is listening, the other one wants that affirmation too. If we are honest, we all want affirmation. That affirmation comes through words. Maybe some of you are about to set out on a new venture and all you are desiring is a push from others to let you know they are rooting for you. What does that support do, or those positive words do for you? They give you the confidence that you can do it. Don't they?

I remember when I was in high school - although I made good grades initially, I struggled with using the correct grammar in English. I had an English teacher who told me and others in the class that we were going to fail English in college if we didn't get our grammar right. I started dreading going to English class. Those negative words began to consume me. Those words kept getting repeated in my mind: "You are going to fail, You are going to fail..." Maybe some of you can relate to this scenario. When I had to write an essay as part of the test, I made all kinds of mistakes. You know what those negative words generated? Fear. It seemed that the harder I tried, the more mistakes I made. I can see that English paper now - A/F: A for content but F for grammar. I was able to get through the class, but for a short time those negative words had robbed me of my confidence. I begin to rehearse those words in my mind to the point that I started believing them. So, when I did graduate from high school and went to college, those negative words followed me.

What do you suppose happened during my freshmen year in college? I struggled in English class. I doubted my written work because I had no trust in my ability. I ended up making a C+ in English which was disappointing. It wasn't that I could not write, but I had heard those negative words so much that I begin to believe them. Again, I had lost my confidence in my ability. I was fearful of making mistakes so I made mistakes. Isn't it unfortunate how those negative words generated fear? I was somehow able to pull it together and started doing much better during my sophomore year in college, but it was a struggle to get there. That incident displays the power of words and the impact they can have on your life.

I also had an instructor in college who recognized my ability and understanding of economics. He occasionally would solicit my input to determine if the lesson concept had been explained clearly. Sometimes this instructor would also grade on a curve, meaning points were added to bring the highest score to a 100. I had some classmates wanting to know what I made to see the maximum number of points that could be added to their grade as some assumed I had made the highest score. I was confident in this class. Why? Because the instructor affirmed me and spoke positive things about me.

Please know that I do believe that we can get to a level of maturity where we can validate and affirm ourselves according to the Word of God. The point I am really trying to emphasize is what negative words can do to people who possibly have not reached the level of maturity necessary to affirm themselves; possibly, none of us ever gets there completely. May we be the ones to allow God to use us to affirm others. Let's speak kindly to one another and uphold one another.

Proverbs 18:21 MSG says, "Words kill, words give life; they're either poison or fruit – you choose."

Wow; think about this scripture. That's influential. This scripture lets us know the power of words. Each day we have the choice and can decide what words we will speak over our lives, over our children, over our spouses, over our family and friends. God wants our words to bring life and strength to each other. On the other hand, Satan wants our words to devour each other. We may not want to deliberately hurt anyone with our words, but if we do not guard what we say, that could very well happen.

"'SPEAK WHEN YOU ARE ANGRY AND YOU WILL MAKE THE BEST SPEECH YOU WILL EVER REGRET'"

This scripture says we choose what we want our words to accomplish. That's why we should not speak when we are angry because if we say hurtful words, those effects could possibly last a lifetime. The scripture says to be quick to hear, slow to speak and slow to anger. The tongue has the power of life and death. Your words can either speak life, or your words can speak death.

There is a quote I read that says, "Speak when you are angry, and you will make the best speech you will ever regret." That's something to think about. Negative words spoken could cause a life of regret. The book of James talks about the tongue, noting that at times we bless God and then curse men made after the likeness of God. James points out that this should not be. Do you think about your words? Do you ask questions like: "Did I overreact to that? Could I have responded better or handled that situation better? Did I speak too soon?" I believe that it is essential to examine our words and think before we speak because, good or bad, our words have consequences.

During my sophomore year in college, I got the opportunity to travel to Westlake Village, California, to work for IBM in their coop program. This was so exciting for me, coming from a small town. IBM paired me up with a roommate and I was hoping that I would have a newfound friend, but the opposite happened. During the first few weeks of getting to know her, she began to express her insecurities about her weight. I began to encourage her but then she began to speak cruelly to me. I really did not know how to respond. I was loss for words. I became miserable.

It got to the point we would drive to and from work together in complete silence. When we would get to her apartment, I would go straight to my designated room I was paying to live in. I remember calling my mom and she said, "San, come home". I didn't want to. This was such an amazing opportunity for me. I didn't want to take the opportunity lightly so I decided to stick it out.

However, one day, my manager decided he wanted to talk to his coop when it was about time to go home. While I was talking to my manager, my roommate called me on the phone stating that she was waiting. Please know that I was only a few minutes late, and the irony is that the day before I had waited for her as she was part of a volleyball tournament, but I understand it was her car. She called me on my phone and said, "I am waiting." I had to tell my manager I had to go.

I ran down the stairs to get in the car. Guess what happened? When I tried to get in the car, she drove off to the end of the street and stopped. She had another girl in the car that she carpooled with so I was totally humiliated. So, what did I do? I walked up to the end of the street and got in the car. See, this was the first time I had been that far away from home. I really did not know what else to do. I felt that her actions and how she had talked to me caused me to feel inferior. I believe I cried all night after that incident. While driving to work the next morning with her, in silence, I continued to process what had happened.

There were two other people in the office I worked in. One of them begin talking to me, and out of nowhere I begin to cry. I did everything to hold my tears back. Of course, they wanted to know what was wrong. Here I was in a big city among strangers. Do I let them know what had happened? I was desperate. Once I shared what had happened, that same day, they reported her to the personnel contact who was responsible for finding coops a place to stay. Next, they told me that I was moving out of that place. Thank God for those guardian angels! I excitedly packed all my bags that night. After I moved out, I was placed with another family. The experience was much better, and I enjoyed the rest of my summer as a coop. The nightmare turned into a happy ending.

Why do I mention this incident? Because she tried to devalue me with words—maybe because of her own insecurities, I don't know. When I have shared this story in the past, I often wonder about her. Even now I think about her as I write this book; did she ever find a place of peace within herself? Did she ever start valuing others with her words? I sure hope she did.

Maybe you have been guilty of this and have sometimes degraded people with words. I just encourage you to repent to God and move forward from here and start from this day forward being an instrument of God valuing people, despite your personal circumstance or situation.

Origin of Words

As we talk about the power of words, it is essential that we look at the book of Genesis. Why? Because here we find the origin of words. Genesis Chapter 1 starts off by saying, "In the beginning, God created heaven and earth." Genesis 1:3 says, "And God said, Let there be light: and there was light." Throughout Genesis Chapter 1 we see these words: "And God said," even to the creation of man. Genesis 1:26-27 says, "And God said, Let us make man in our image, after our likeness: and let them have dominion over the fish of the sea ... So God created man in his own image, in the image of God created he him; male and female created he them." What is it that we see in this chapter? That everything came as a result of God speaking. Everything God spoke came into existence. Words cannot get any more powerful than that.

Genesis 1:28 goes on to say, "And God blessed them, and God said unto them, Be fruitful, and multiply, and replenish the earth, and subdue it: and have dominion over the fish of the sea..." Here we have God giving man authority over the earth to rule it, and this authority came with inspiring words. Think about it. If God gave man authority over the earth and God used words to create everything, then if God's Words are powerful, so are ours.

Matthew Chapter 8 talks about an officer who ask Jesus to heal his servant. Jesus agreed to come but the officer responded by saying, "Lord, I am not worthy that thou shouldest come under my roof: but speak the word only and my servant shall be healed." This officer understood the power of words. He knew that Jesus had the power to heal his servant and that the power could be exercised by just speaking the word. Because God's Word is powerful and enriching, it is so important to decree God's Word over our lives. To say, "I will believe what God says about me." God's Word in you is powerful and liberating, but Satan's words have the opposite effect. God wants us to decree his Word which causes great things to manifest in our lives.

What if we went around declaring only what God says? How many people's lives would we bless? There is a story in Mark 4 where the disciples were in the boat and a storm came. Jesus was asleep in the boat. They woke Jesus up and asked whether he cared that they were going to perish. Jesus arose and rebuked the storm by saying: "Peace, be still." There go words again. The storm calmed when Jesus spoke to it. It is time we realize the authority that we have to use God's Word. God's Word is powerful and our words are powerful. What can we say, even to fear? "Peace, be still."

"IT'S TIME WE REALIZE THE AUTHORITY THAT WE HAVE TO USE GOD'S WORD"

Let's look at the scriptures in Matthew Chapter 4, when Jesus was led by the spirt into the wilderness to be tempted of the devil. Jesus had been fasting 40 days and 40 nights and the scripture said he was hungry. The devil came to Him and challenged who He was by saying, "If thou be the Son of God, command that these stones be made bread." Jesus responded, "Man shall not live by bread alone but by every word that proceedeth out of the mouth of God." Jesus was ready for any temptation Satan tried to come at Him with. The key is that Jesus noted, "It is written". That is how we defeat the enemy by knowing what God says. Satan tried to trick Jesus, but he couldn't. Satan's goal is to try to trick us into submitting to his lies and deception, but we are to pattern our lives after Jesus. Satan may have tricked Adam and Eve, but he was not ready for the Son of God!

In the story about the life of Stamatis Moraitis that I shared with you in the Chapter *Influence of the Mind*, Stamatis spoke positive words over his life by saying, "I will die happy," despite the bad report from the medical doctors. He made his mind up and then he spoke optimism. He could have looked at his situation and spoken doom and gloom, but he didn't. He decided to enjoy life, no matter how long or how short it turned out to be. You see how powerful you are when your mind and positive words work together? We must be reminded of the importance of creating life with our words. Let's use the power that God has given us to make a positive impact for the Kingdom of God by affirming and building each other up with the powerful Word of God. Yes, words can hurt, but they can also heal and set free if we follow God's direction.

In my leadership position on my job, I have often been told that I know how to have a conversation that leaves a person unoffended, even during some of the most difficult discussions. You know why? Because those meetings have the purest intentions of wanting to see others succeed.

I encourage you to try this experiment one day: Make a conscientious note of your words throughout the day. Note what you said. Note how you said it. Later that day, look at all the words you spoke. Prayerfully you used words to build others up. But if you didn't, repent and ask God to help you.

I read a story about a group of frogs who were travelling through the woods, when two of the frogs fell into a pit. The other frogs saw how deep the pit was and told the two frogs they would never get out. It initially seemed as though the two frogs ignored the comments and kept trying. Negative words were coming out of the mouths of the other frogs, telling them to give up.

One frog finally succumbed to the negative words and gave up and died. The enduring frog continued to jump as high as he could and finally made it out. Once he made it out, the other frogs asked whether he'd heard their negative words. He let them know that he was deaf and had assumed they were encouraging him. (Susan Holsinger, February 24, 2021). This story again demonstrates the power of words. I encourage you to be that frog who is deaf to negative words and refuse to give up, regardless of how deep the pit may seem. You can do all things through Christ which strengthens you.

I enjoy hearing my little grandson sing the song "Faith Talk" by Mike Todd. Parts of the song says, "My family will be healed that's my faith talk...My kids will love Jesus that's my faith talk..." He enjoys singing this song as all the family dance around him, encouraging him to sing. We all begin to laugh when he sings: "I will pray for my wife that's my faith talk." But what do you think our positive words are doing to my grandson? They are building him up, encouraging and empowering him. He loves it and we love it. Remember - faith talk is believing God's Word and saying what God says, and that is power!

One of my favorite songs is "Released" by Donald Lawrence. If you have not heard it, I encourage you to listen to that song. He reminds you in the song that you are officially released. The song builds you up and tells you of God's plans for your life. It is time to release your fears to God for you don't have to be afraid. God will deliver you from whatever challenges you are facing because He has ordained you to soar.

Now that we know what fear is and have talked about the influence of the mind and the power of words, let's take the First Step towards deliverance by completing the "Release My Fear (s)" Worksheet.

First Step: Release My Fear(s) Worksheet

Release your Fear(s). I encourage you to be honest before God. Release them all. I believe confession is good for the soul. It doesn't matter how many. It's time to be transparent. It's time to be free.

God I Release my fears before you:

1._____
_____
_____
_____
_____

2._____
_____
_____
_____
_____

3._____
_____
_____

WHAT IS THE ROOT OF FEAR?

I have provided insight through divine revelation from God, to me, as to what fear is, but I believe it is also important to discuss the root or origin of fear in more depth. Origin means the beginning.

Ezekiel 28:15 says, "Thou wast perfect in thy ways from the day that thou wast created, till iniquity was found in thee."

You know who this scripture is talking about? It is talking about Satan. This, among other scriptures, explains where Satan's ruin began. When pride entered his heart he became that old serpent, called the devil Satan. What happened? He wanted to be like God, but everything about him was corrupt. He was totally evil.

In Luke Chapter 10, Jesus sent seventy of his disciples out to do the work of the Lord. When they returned to Jesus, they said to Him that even the devils were subject to unto them through Jesus' name. Jesus then pointed out to them that He beheld Satan as lightning falling from heaven. What happened? Satan with his corrupt nature was thrown out of heaven. So where did he go? Revelations tells us that he was cast unto the earth and his angels were cast out with him. He is referred to as the god of this world according to 2 Corinthians 4:4, who has blinded the minds of them which believe not. From this we see that he is the root of all fear because he is the root of all evil.

I would like to note that the Bible does say that we are to fear God, but that type of fear refers to reverence and adoration. But fear from Satan is evil and corrupt. Know this, Satan is a fallen angel who wanted to be like God. He wanted the authority that God has. He had no place in Heaven so his desire is to make people miserable on Earth. Satan hates us and he hates that God has extended grace to us. He knows his time of being god of this world will soon come to an end. He is eternally damned and his final destination is the lake of fire.

1 Peter 5:8 says, "Be sober, be vigilant; because your adversary the devil, as a roaring lion, walketh about, seeking whom he may devour." We must take note that he is always trying to imitate the power and authority that God has. Here he is going around as a roaring lion, but he is not the Lion of Judah as Jesus is referred to as, signifying Jesus' majesty and power. Satan is our enemy and he wants to devour us. He is also referred to as our adversary. That's an opponent. The Word of God is telling

us to be alert. God wants us to be watchful. In fact, the Word tells us to watch and pray.

John 16:13 says, "These things I have spoken unto you, that in me ye might have peace. In the world ye shall have tribulation: but be of good cheer; I have overcome the world". This scripture is powerful and encouraging. Although tribulation, distress and suffering are from the god of this world, Jesus tells us He has overcome. And because He has overcome, we have overcome.

I used to enjoy watch boxing matches. I remember watching a boxing match once and it looked as if one boxer was definitely going to knock the other one out. His opponent took one punch after another. Again, I just knew there was going to be a knockout. But he never was able to knock him out. After the fight, the commentator asked the one who kept throwing the punches, "Why couldn't you take him out with all those punches?" He replied, "The harder I hit him, the stronger he got." Wow, that's powerful. Have you been dealing with one punch from fear after another?

Genesis 3:15 says, "And I will put enmity between thee and the woman, and between thy seed and her seed; it shall bruise thy head, and thou shalt bruise his heel." These are the Words of God after Satan had enticed Eve to eat of the forbidden fruit. Did you know that God is talking about Jesus in part of this scripture? Jesus came to earth through the seed of a woman.

There is opposition between Jesus and Satan. The Bible says, he (Satan) shalt bruise his heel, meaning it was predestined that Jesus would be made sin for us and shed His blood for all mankind. He gave His life so that all who would come unto Him would have eternal life. Jesus' death was temporal because Jesus went to the cross and rose from the grave three days later declaring power over all the works of Satan. But what is God saying to serpent (Satan) when he says, "It shall bruise thy head."?

Jesus would bruise the head of Satan. Here God is declaring Satan's final fate. Jesus defeated Satan when He went to the cross. When Jesus shed His blood, He took back the authority that Adam and Eve had lost through disobedience. I like to think about it this way. How do you kill a serpent? With a blow to the head. That's what Jesus did, He gave the final blow to Satan. That tells us that the god of this world may throw his punches, but they are dead on arrival.

It's time to deal with the root of fear and destroy that fruit. When Jesus cursed the fig tree in Matthew Chapter 21, he said, "No fruit shall grow on you henceforth." What happened? The fig tree withered away. Are you ready for fear to wither away? Say, "I am ready."

I remember years ago I was dealing with something and I went to God about it. To be honest, I have forgotten what it specifically was. But what has stayed with me after all these years is the intense desire I felt to get out of that situation. I am positive it had something to do with fear. I did not want to go through that test or take the punches Satan was throwing at me. After much praying, I felt the Lord speaking to me, saying: "I will get you out for now but you are going to have to pass this test." I guess you could say I was not ready to get in the boxing ring. I was so glad to get out of the test that maybe unconsciously I said, "Okay God". God was trying to warn me that skipping the test was not an option. Let me ask you a question: How many tests have you tried to skip? It's personal. The truth is I did have to go through it again, because God wanted me to pass the test. He wanted me to see that He was able to protect me and guide me. I did not have to be afraid, because He was right there in the ring of life with me. I did not have to be afraid of Satan or anyone. He wanted me to trust Him. When the test came up again, I went through it and passed it because God is so faithful.

That is the point I believe Jesus was making to Paul regarding the thorn in his flesh. If you are unfamiliar with this passage in the Bible, read 2 Corinthians 12: 6-9. It is a powerful story, as Paul asked Jesus not once, not twice, but three times, regarding removing the thorn in his flesh. There are many theologians who debate about what

"THE TEMPTATION OF FEAR DOES NOT HAVE TO RULE YOUR LIFE"

Paul's thorn in the flesh was. I will not enter that debate, but the point I am making is that when Paul came to Jesus regarding the thorn in the flesh, Jesus said: "My grace is sufficient. My strength is made perfect in weakness". We can rest in God's sufficient grace. I encourage you to go ahead and take the test. You will pass it. 100% guaranteed. God wants us to believe His Word and know He is able to deliver us. 1 Corinthians 10:13 lets us know that God will not allow us to be tempted above that which we are able to handle, but with that temptation make a way of escape that we may be able to endure it.

That temptation of fear does not have to rule your life. Do I need to say it again? Fear does not need to rule your life. One of my aunts once said that 90% of the things she worried about never came to pass. If there is truth to that, and I believe there is, it shows that we spend our life worried about most things that will not ever happen. Digest that for a moment. Look back over your life. Compare what you feared to what actually happened.

The scripture says, "And if God cares so wonderfully for flowers that are here today and gone tomorrow, won't he more surely care for you?" (Matthew 6:30 Living Bible). Isn't it liberating to know that God cares for you? You are His creation. You are made in His image and he loves you with an everlasting love. Isaiah 43:2 says, "When thou passest through the waters, I will be with thee; and through the rivers, they shall not overflow thee: when thou walkest through the fire, thou shalt not be burned; neither shall the flame kindle upon thee". Be encouraged by this scripture that whatever you are facing, God is with you. Let us also be constantly reminded that although Satan may be throwing his punches, stay in the ring with God - because Jesus has given Satan the final blow, and that is a knockout!

HOW FEAR GAINED ACCESS
INTO MY LIFE

I believe fear gained access in my life as a little girl. I was fortunate to be raised in a family where I had two loving parents and seven brothers and sisters. I believe eight is enough! However, during my childhood, it seemed as if my mom constantly was sick. She was in and out of the hospital and I constantly worried about her. I would find myself wishing she was healthy like other moms.

You can only imagine the agony caused on a little girl who constantly lived a life worried about her mom. I didn't really let others know. I did not even let my mom know, but I believe that constantly worrying about my mom was the root of my fear. My ultimate fear became the fear of sickness and disease. When my siblings got sick, I worried. I took on a lot of worry as a little girl.

Maybe God allowed it so I could one day share with others the hope and healing promises of the Almighty God, and how he set me free. If you are dealing with fear, I advise you to do a self-examination and determine what was or is at the root of your fear - and please be honest with yourself. That honesty holds the keys to your deliverance, to your peace and to your victory from fear.

God called me into the ministry in my 30's. The week I was to preach my first message, my mom was with me as I was taking her back and forth to the doctor because she was having health issues. Later that week I was scheduled to preach my first sermon. I still preached that night but I had to deal with fear, worry and anxiety. See, I was saved, but I did not understand taking authority over fear (the enemy). After preaching my first message, I continued to accept preaching engagements and my mom's health issues continued. I did go ahead and preach so I did not allow the fear to immobilize me to the point where I did not do anything, but boy, did I want to turn opportunities down! That's what fear from the enemy does. Satan wants to paralyze you from doing the work, of God. Don't let him. Think about it - if we give the enemy that much power with fear, what about the power we could tap into with faith in God? I did not understand it then, but I do now. Thank God for the victory. Start taking your rightful place today and tap into your faith in God.

I was raised in church literally all my life. I heard many sermons, but I did not hear anyone

talking about dealing with fear so I suffered si-
lently. That fear gripped me. My mind became
flooded with the fear of what might happen.
Unfortunately, the fear seed was planted. It took
years for me to finally know that I was free. See,
you can be saved and still allow the enemy to
cause havoc in your life. Now I realize that during those years in my life, Satan was able to torment me with fear, although saved, because I
was living in the soulish realm (where my mind
and emotions ruled) versus living in the spirit.
Living in the soulish realm caused me to deal
with the enemy from a position of defeat rather
than victory, so in my adulthood, I found myself fearing everything. If my toe hurt, I found
myself thinking, "What is this?" I remember going to the doctor because I was concerned about
my chest. He did an X-ray and pointed out that
what I was feeling was just my chest bone. It
sounds insane or maybe funny right now, but if
that demonic force is trying to control you and
keep you in fear, then it becomes tormenting.

Satan is using fear, anxiety and worry to torment so many people's lives. Unfortunately,
many allow him to do this by entertaining
those demonic thoughts from him as I once did,
because we fail to rest in the promises and
peace of God. Many times, we fail to do this

through ignorance, not really understanding what is happening. What is the enemy tormenting you with right now? You do not have to take it anymore. Say, "Enough is enough."

You cannot live like that

I remember on my job one day, years ago, talking to a lady whose daughter was in remission from some form of cancer. I begin talking to her and my fears became evident. She looked at me as sincerely as I believe she could and said, "You cannot live like that". She was absolutely right. Although the fear was deeply rooted, I felt a release as I thought about her remarks: "You cannot live like that". And I will say to you, if you are living in fear, "You cannot live like that."

The benefits of fear

Maybe we need to look at the benefits of fear. Of course, I say that sarcastically. But we allow fear to rule us as if there are benefits. Psalm 103: 1-2 says, "Bless the LORD, O my soul: and all that is within me, bless his holy name. Bless the LORD, O my soul, and forget not all his benefits". God is the only one that has the true goods and benefits for our lives. There are no benefits to fear from Satan. Worry, anxiety,

and torment, to name but a few, are only designed to rob you of the victory that Jesus paid
for us. Continue to say: "God has not given me a
spirit of fear." Say it to the point that faith arises
in your spirit, so strongly that your faith in
God's Word makes the enemy tremble as he has
tried to make you tremble. Remember, we fight
not against flesh and blood, but against spiritual wickedness in high places.

I remember once dealing with the spirit of
depression. I know now even that stemmed
from the fear that was lurking its ugly head
somewhere in my life. I dealt with that depression for approximately six months. I stood on
the Word of God. I remember that every day my
husband would go to work and my kids would
go to school. After everyone had left, that spirit
of depression was there, staring me in the face
and determined to torment me.

I truly have empathy for those who are battling with depression. If you are, I encourage
you to get the help you need. Seek the Holy
Spirit for guidance. I did not get on medication
but I am not opposed to seeking doctor's assis-
tance if needed.

The point I am really trying to make is that I
stood against it. I battled that evil force with the
Word of God. I recited scriptures, I spoke my

deliverance and I stood on God's Word. See, I did not focus on the emotion, but on the Word of God. So, what happened? It was miraculous! One morning, I woke up and the depression was gone. That tormenting spirit had left. The enemy can stay only so long after hearing the powerful Word of God. I threw one word at him after another. Hallelujah!

God said to resist the devil and he will flee. I resisted that evil force using the Word of God, and it had to leave. I encourage you to pull out your Spiritual weapons today and use them. Use them from a position of victory. We have already overcome by the blood of the lamb and the words of our testimony. Resist that fear to-day!

A Personal Story:

"San, I wish you would pray for Wynn." Those were the words from my mom. We'd had a close family member diagnosed with lung cancer. This family member was also my mom's best friend, and my mom wanted me to pray for her healing. The problem was that I was full of fear; however, I was feeling the heaviness of my mom's request. I did not realize totally at that time how my mom so believed in my prayers to God. This brings tears to my eyes just thinking about that memory.

You see, while I was in college, my mom started losing weight and she expressed to our family: "Look at me, I am losing weight". I truly believe in prayer, but I know Satan wanted me to hear what my mom said because of my fear. Immediately I began to pray for my mom. I remember one day while home from college I was in another room reading my Bible, and mom came running down the hall saying, "He touched me, San, God touched me, I am healed!" I said, "Mom, let's pray," and we thanked God. Mom started back gaining her weight and we rejoiced. Later I found out that my mom had found a lump in her breast and Dad had told her to leave it alone and not touch it. They had been praying for healing. Thank God He did!

Subsequently, my mom's best friend Wynn was diagnosed with lung cancer. My mom began to press me–"San, I wish you would go and pray for Wynn." Believe me I wanted her healed; she was like an aunt to me. However, I was looking from a natural perspective as I had seen the effects this dreadful disease had caused on so many people. As my mom continued to press me, I finally succumbed. I remember going to my grandmother's house and watching a family movie that night. I said a prayer and went to bed. I got up that morning and walked over to my mom best friend's home. We were blessed that our families lived in close proximity to each other.

For that moment, I denounced my fear and I walked over there and begin to pray with boldness. I believe I must have prayed so loud that my other grandmother came out of her house and stood in the street while I prayed. I felt the presence of God, His anointing, His power, but to my disappointment, she was not physically healed. Although I knew the presence of God was present to heal, I know now that I lacked the wisdom to engage in conversations to speak life to her. See, I didn't know the struggles she was dealing with after the prayer, and what words she was saying or how Satan was trying to invade her thought life. You may be believing healing and it is yours, but we need wisdom from God to focus on how to receive it and keep it.

The Bible says that Satan left Jesus for a season after being tempted. God said, "My people are destroyed for lack of knowledge." We have to build our knowledge on the Word of God and know the precious promises that are ours. How do you respond when the enemy comes back and says, "You will not get that promotion; You are not healed; God does not hear you?" These are examples of tormenting lies that he wants us to believe - but whose report will we believe? Declare that you will believe the report of the Lord. We are to resist every evil thought of the enemy. God wants us to stand on what He said. Amen!

"DECLARE THAT YOU WILL BELIEVE THE REPORT OF THE LORD. WE ARE TO RESIST EVERY EVIL THOUGHT OF THE ENEMY"

I have other examples of fear, but I shared these as they were part of the root of my fear. Thank God for deliverance. Remember, address the root and you will destroy the fruit. Maybe your fear is something else. Whatever it may be,

God wants to deliver you and set you free. He does not want you in bondage. There are many types of fears, but all fears from Satan are demonic and evil and are aimed at stealing your peace. Hasn't Satan stolen enough? Haven't you given him enough? Now that you know the truth, what are you going to do? Come out of that cage of bondage and be free today. Say to that tormenting sprit: "You will no longer rule me because whom the Son has set free is free indeed. God has set me free!"

You may be asking the question: Can I live absent from fear? I say Yes, you can. You may feel the emotions of fear but, as I said, fear is much more than an emotion - it is a demonic force from Satan, and you do not have to let that demonic force control your life anymore. God said, "I will keep you in perfect peace, whose mind is stayed on Him."

What have you set your mind on? Change your mindset. Is it possible that you are one thought away from complete deliverance? Yes! Again, Philippians 4:8 says: "Finally, brethren, whatsoever things are true, whatsoever things are honest, whatsoever things are just, whatsoever things are pure, whatsoever things are lovely, whatsoever things are of good report; if there be any virtue, and if there be any praise, think on these things."

God is calling us to have a fear-free life. That sounds good, doesn't it? It is ours. Jesus said that He will never leave us or forsake us, even to the ends of the world. It doesn't mean that we won't have to deal with negative emotions or that Satan will not tempt us to fear. But when we understand the authority we have, the plans God has for us, and we know that He has our best interests at heart and he never meant for us to live in tormenting fear, than THAT is freedom!

An emergency miracle

The fear of sickness and disease appeared to invade a good portion of my life. There were other doors in my life opened to fear; particularly when driving. I loved going to church, but unfortunately, I was not the best driver in my earlier years. The truth of the matter is that I feared merging into ongoing traffic. I can say that God has now delivered me from that fear. But I can relate to those who are dealing with that phobia of driving.

After graduating from college, one particular Sunday, I remember driving my sister's car to church. I was really enjoying the church services but during church services, the enemy was bombarding my mind: "You are enjoying church but you have to drive back home." Upon leaving church, as I got on the interstate, I begin to merge too soon into ongoing traffic which caused the car behind me to swerve to keep from hitting me. As a result, the car started going sideways down the interstate going seemingly at 50 to 60 mph. This was not a time for a long prayer. This was not a time to fear. I said something like, "God, straighten that car up. I don't want that on my conscious." I don't even know whether I said please or not. I was desperate for what I call an emergency miracle. We must know God is performing these every day. God was faithful and heard my prayer - the angels were on their posts. I literally watched that car straighten up on the interstate after going seemingly full speed sideways. This was definitely an amazing miracle that I witnessed before my eyes as the people in the car were okay. When the car finally straightened up and I was about to pass them, in the correct lane of course, I could feel their eyes staring at me and possibly calling me a few choice words. I didn't care. I dared not look. I was just so grateful they were okay.

God is truly faithful and He protects us and watches over us every day. Know that your journey with God can be free of fear, anxiety and worry. Isaiah 43:1 says in part, "...Fear not: for I have redeemed thee, I have called thee by thy name; thou art mine." That's powerful. God reminds us we are His and He surely will take care of us. For those of you that have children, what would you do if someone messed with your children or even a family member (stay spiritual)? The point is you would protect them - and will not God protect his children who diligently seek His guidance?

I share my personal struggles and stories because I desire that people be set free. Sharing personal struggles can be the catalyst to help others gain hope. Hope in seeing you made it. You survived. You kept the faith. You are free. I do believe in being led by the Spirit of God when it comes to sharing. If God leads you to share a personal struggle to help someone, I encourage you to do it. Remember, if we can help somebody along the way our living shall not be in vain.

I like the scripture in John 11 where Jesus told the grave clothes to free Lazarus and let him go. I can only imagine what that scene must have looked like. I am using my spiritual imagination as I see God saying today: "Fear, free my child and let him go. I see fear releasing you like those grave clothes had to let Lazarus go." Amen!

We must realize, fear is real and it is trying to cripple so many of God's people. Sometimes we don't want to admit it as we may appear to look weak. I understand that, dealing with my own personal struggles, but God said, "Let the weak say I am strong." I have come to see, when something is exposed, then deliverance can come.

Some may say "Just read your Bible if you are dealing with fear." If that alone was the cure, I would not be writing this book as I would not have a point of reference with experiences with fear. I was and still am a fervent reader of the Word of God. See, the truth of the matter is that reading the Word of God and knowing how to apply it are what bring deliverance. I can read all day long, but if I don't apply it and stand on the promises of God, I cannot be free. If you are driving to a destination with a tank full of gas, you will never get there until you turn the ignition with your key and place your foot on the accelerator. It's time to turn the key away from fear, place your foot on the accelerator towards faith, and trust in God. Are you ready to leave fear behind? I believe you are ready. I believe you are reading this book because you are. I believe you have had enough of fear. Praise God! Keep reading.

I extend Christ to you

As you have noticed in reading this book, I have mentioned a lot of scriptures, so the assumption is that this book is speaking to Christians (those that have accepted Jesus as their Lord and Savior). If you have not, I extend the invitation to you. Jesus is your door to freedom and your deliverance from fear. "For God so loved the world, that he gave his only begotten Son, that whosoever believeth in him should not perish, but have everlasting life." (John 3:16).

Please say this simple prayer: "Jesus, please come into my life. Please forgive me of my sins. I believe you are the Son of God and that you gave your life that I might be saved." If you said this prayer and believe it, you are now part of the body of Christ. To assist with your growth, I encourage you to ask God to help you find a local church. Welcome to the body of Christ!

Now that you know that Satan is the root of all fear, it's time to take the next step by completing the Root of My Fear(s) worksheet as you are another step closer to a fear-free life.

The Root of my Fear(s) Worksheet

Now it is time to do a self-examination and list how fear gained access into your life. Don't rush through this. Take your time and complete it. There is no condemnation. You may have been a child like me when fear started. I encourage you to really think about it. Again, transparency is the key. God already knows, but deliverance comes when we are honest with God and ourselves. Ask the Holy Spirit to help you and expose anything that has been hidden. Know this - that you are another step closer to being free.

God, I acknowledge that fear started in my life when...

_____

_____

_____

_____

_____

_____

_____

_____

HOW TO GET RID OF FEAR?

You are now at the final section in the book. The important question is, how can you get rid of fear? Throughout the book, I have provided you with encouraging words and actions for you to follow to help you get rid of fear, but I would like to elaborate even more.

You may ask me, "But what got you to the place of No More Fear?" I wish I could say it was in my 20s, 30s or even 40s. No. It was in the beginning of my 50s when I was diagnosed with breast cancer. Yes, fear was ready and waiting to torment me. See, I have learned we can be the best teacher, instructor or even preacher until we have to be the student. We have the best advice on how to raise children, until we become parents. We have the best advice how to trust God, until we have to trust God.

Despite my inner fear and turmoil, for most of my life, God had used me to encourage people. No doubt I believe if the Pope came to town, I could have provided an encouraging word, but I found myself like David entering into a place where I had to encourage myself. I fervently pray it does not take you that long to say No More Fear. God does not want you to suffer in silence and neither do I. I pray you declare today, No More!

Satan's all bark but our words give him bite

What steps did I take? I have come to learn that the best way to deal with fear is to face it. You must acknowledge it and stand against it. You may even need to speak to that evil force of fear and declare, "You will no longer torment me. I have had enough". Isn't your peace worth fighting for? Ephesians 6 says to put on the whole armour of God that you

> **"THE BEST WAY TO DEAL WITH FEAR IS TO FACE IT."**

may be able to stand in the evil day. I have come to a place in my life that I understand the importance of wearing the armour of God. I believe that you will come to that revelation as well.

Matthew 24 says if the goodman of the house had known at what time the thief would come, he would not have allowed his house to be broken into. When we allow Satan to make us fearful, we are giving him access to take residence in our house (our mind and emotions) where he tries to rule. It is time to put that bully out.

I remember that when I was in college, one of the girls on the campus went around trying to bully everyone, especially other girls. I was a Resident Assistant at the time and everyone came to me with problems; however, one day the bully harassed the wrong person. What happened? The bully came to me crying, regarding someone picking on her. Yes, there was that one brave girl who had had enough. I realized then that the bully was all bark and no bite. If only we could see the enemy like that! Satan is all bark and only our words, and our fears, when acted upon, give him bite. I found myself going to the brave girl and asking her to leave the bully alone. We both looked at each other and began to laugh. She said, "I will not bother her anymore." I didn't hear of another instance of the bullying after that.

I want to encourage you that although Satan may have caused you to be fearful, Proverbs 31 reminds us that you shall laugh in the days to come. This simple story has revelation in it and is so powerful. As long as no one challenged the bully, the bullying continued to cause havoc in others' lives, but once someone challenged the bully, she retreated. That's what Jesus did for us. Colossians 2:15 Amplified Bible: "When He had disarmed the rulers and authorities (those supernatural forces of evil operating against us), He made a public example of them (exhibiting them as captives in His triumphal procession), having triumphed over them through the cross." He triumphed over Satan and put him to an open shame. Although man was broken and condemned due to sin, Jesus bought our redemption back. He challenged the bully and the bully (Satan) retreated and not only retreated but was defeated! Jesus has given us the power to overcome anything Satan brings our way. The scripture says that God's power lives in every believer. It's time to command that bully flee!

Authority over Satan

Do you see it now? Do you see we have the power and authority over Satan because of what Jesus did at the cross? Let's stop letting the bark control us. God said, "I will never leave thee or forsake thee, even to the ends of the world." He has triumphed over Satan and so have we. Hallelujah! Fear cannot torment you. Fear has no authority over you – not God's child. You have the victory. Isaiah 59:19 says that when the enemy comes against us like a flood, He will lift up a standard against the enemy. God wants us to trust Him and His Word, so take authority over fear.

You say, "It is easier said than done." I understand that thought process, but if you are led by the spirit of God and not by the soulish realm, then you must know that you will come out triumphantly. We must spend time with God to replace fear with faith. Get you some scriptures. Meditate on those scriptures. Say them even if your emotions are speaking to the contrary. Keep saying them. Know the power of your words.

Again, I lived a life of suppressing inner fear rather than facing it. No one told me to face it - or rather I did not hear this advice with my spiritual ears, so I spent many years living that life of suppressing my fears. I don't want that to happen to you. You can be delivered and set free today. I finally realized that my emotions could not cripple me with fear unless I let them. It's time for you to realize that too.

I often think about women, including myself, in the waiting room for a mammogram – numerous times. It seems to take a long time, especially when others come after you and leave before you. I know those times all so well. Those times try to create fear, but for me, No More!

Maybe you are a woman or even a man waiting to hear the results of a test or doctor's report - I encourage you to hold on to your faith. It is not a feeling but a position. I stand with faith, not fear. I stand with God's Word, not Satan's word. What gets rid of your fear is really believing that God's promises are for you and your family. Faith is more powerful than fear if it is exercised. Just like we have exercised fear, God wants us to exercise faith. Let the exercising of your fear be in your past now. Say what faith says. Faith says, "No weapon formed against me will

"FAITH IN GOD IS TO ALLOW HIS WORDS TO COME OUT OF YOUR MOUTH..."

prosper." Faith says, "By His stripes I am healed." Faith says, "If God be for me who can be against me?" Faith says, "I will live and not die and declare the glory of the Lord."

Faith in God is to allow His Words to come out of your mouth and uproot every tormenting lie of the enemy. It is time to allow faith to overrule fear. Faith in God is more powerful, as He has given every man the measure of faith. Know that the key to your deliverance has always been inside of you, because greater is He that is in you than he that is in the world. Make up your mind that you are going to follow the

Word of God. Take what Ephesians 6 says to be strong in the Lord and in the power of his might.

At this point in the book, I pray you are saying, "I have had enough. Fear will not torment me anymore and definitely not for the rest of my life. I refuse to be tormented." Say, "No More!" Keep repeating this to the point you are ready to deal with that bully who has only a bark and no bite. Don't you see now that our words can give voice to the bark, or they can silence the bark. Jesus said, "Who can convict me of sin?" Are we allowing Satan, a defeated foe, to cause us to fear? Say a resounding, "NO!"

MY FAITH IN ACTION

What happened to me? December 2015, I go to the doctor for my regular mammogram. I hear the words, "We see something." I talked with a radiologist who said: "I don't think it's anything, but we need a biopsy." I was somewhat okay because I'd had a biopsy before, so I scheduled the biopsy and waited on the results. But this time, after the biopsy, I was told these words: "You have cancer."

That word cancer began to ring in my ears. Fear tried to grip me, torment me, and put me in a very dark place. I said to myself, "I have two daughters and a husband." I knew fear wanted to put me in an early grave, almost saying, "I got you now. You can't suppress me anymore." Fear was talking to me and it was throwing one deceptive thought at me after another. Everything imaginable was going through my mind, and besides all that I had to go home and share this doctor's report.

How was I going to do that? How was I to tell my husband, and especially my daughters? How was I to hold it together? This was an ultimate fear for me that I now had to face. I felt backed against the wall. I could no longer suppress the inner turmoil. No - I had no choice now, I had to face it.

I remember thinking, "I have to get myself together before I arrive home with this disturbing news." As I was driving home, those evil thoughts and vain imaginations were bombarding my mind. For a short period of time, I felt out of control. At least, I knew my thoughts were.

I will never forget that day as long as I live. While driving home to share the news with my family regarding the doctor's diagnosis, again my emotions initially appeared to be all over the place. All types of thoughts were bombarding my mind, trying to make me feel I was trapped but, wait, all of a sudden, it seemed out of nowhere, peace came over me. It was an indescribable peace. I felt an overwhelming calmness that I can't explain. It was if I had left the car I was driving (or that Satan was trying to drive) and I was in a spiritual convertible driven by God. I was no longer afraid. I was driving and I was no longer fearful. The demonic thoughts were no longer bombarding my mind and I was no longer feeling a sense of hopelessness. Joy was fueling my heart and mind. I realized then I was not in this by myself; no, I was riding in a spiritual convertible designed by God just for me. I was in the presence of God and I was loving it. I saw I was not in Satan's space anymore, and He definitely could not stay in mine.

Satan was in trouble now because Jesus had stepped onto the scene. Jesus was with me now. Jesus was driving and I was relaxing in His ever-abiding peace. I want to use my Southern accent here. It felt good ya'll! I understood now what a lady who had cancer once said to me: "Sandra, I knew if I could get through it, I was going to be okay." Fear had lost its grip and could no longer control me. I too knew I was going to get through it. I knew I was going to be okay. I was free.

When I made it home, I was able to share the doctor's report with such calmness that I even amazed myself. God had the reins to my life and I knew I was safe because I knew my destiny was in God's hands. From my own spiritual wisdom (from God), I knew that the enemy was not through and was going to try to steal this wonderful peace that I was now walking in. Keep in mind that I had only received the prognosis, not the steps that I was about to take in this journey.

I knew Satan was going to try to test my trust in God. So, what did I do? I found healing scriptures in the Word of God and I read and declared them faithfully every day. I also kept a journal of these scriptures in God's Word that brought me peace and comfort. I still have that journal today, as it is a constant reminder how God saw me through that difficult time in my life. One scripture that I read faithfully everyday was 1 Peter 2:24, which states, "Who his own self bare our sins in his own body on the tree, that we being dead to sins, should live unto righteousness: by whose stripes ye were healed." I also read Isaiah 53:4-5, "Surely he hath borne our grief, and carried our sorrows; yet we did esteem him stricken, smitten of God, and afflicted. But he was wounded for our transgressions, he was bruised for our iniquities: the chastisement of our peace was upon him, and with his stripes we are healed."

I knew these two scriptures among several others held the keys to my healing and to my deliverance. Why? Because the stripes Jesus took on his back paved the way for my healing, for your healing, for our deliverance. The truth of the matter is that these scriptures became my breakfast, lunch and dinner. You may ask me, "What does that mean?" Most of us eat physical food three times a day. Just like we need physical food, we also need spiritual food.

Proverbs Chapter 4 tells us that God's Word is life to them that find them and health to all our flesh. After reading these scriptures over and over I begin to feel I could get through anything. I had my spiritual nourishment. They renewed my strength and hope in the powerful promises of God. They brought life to me. I saw my miracle. I saw myself healed. Each day I knew I was getting stronger and stronger in my faith. I declared out loud every day the promises that were mine according to the Word of God. I made those declarations. I made it personal by applying those scriptures to my life, and by speaking them over my life. I believed those promises from God's Word were for me. They were mine.

That's what God wants us to do. We are His children and He wants His children to receive all that He has for them. Please know that whatever you are going through, there is a Word from God over that situation. The Bible says Jesus did not leave one stone unturned - meaning He took care of it all. He knew what we needed and when we would need it.

During this time in my life, I also set aside time every day to meditate. I pondered over those scriptures that I was speaking over my life. I made it personal; I applied it to myself. I reflected on people in the Bible that Jesus had healed. Joshua 1:8 tells us the importance of keeping God's Word before our eyes and meditating on it day and night. That's what I did. I thought about God's Word. Oxford Language defines meditation as to "Think deeply or focus one's mind for a period of time, in silence or with the aid of chanting, for religious or spiritual purposes or as a method of relaxation." When I meditated on God's promises to me, it was a method of relaxation as I continued to rest in Him. See, meditating on God's promises and focusing on them kept me protected from any evil thought from Satan. Think about it this way I am currently on a journey of eating healthier foods. I am sometimes tempted to eat unhealthy foods; however, when I resist eating the wrong foods and go ahead and eat the healthy foods, once I am full then I cannot be tempted. Why? Because I am no longer hungry. I became full of God's Word. There was no room for unhealthy words from Satan. Why? I was full of the good stuff!

Every night my immediate family and I met to pray, praise, and worship God. I encourage you to find yourself a support group who will commit to pray for you each and every day. It is not about the size. In fact, Jesus says in Matthew, "Where two or three are gathered together in my name, I am in the midst." You and one more person with Jesus in the midst become power. I know that my immediate family probably had their own support group to encourage them. As we met every night, we thanked God for answering our prayers. We declared my healing. I remember my son-in-law asking me, "Mother, what do you want us to do? How do you want us to pray?" I provided specific instructions. I let them know what I was specifically praying and believing God for.

During this time, I continued doing everything I normally did – one thing being shopping with my daughters. Maybe I did a little extra shopping. Retail therapy was good for me. At times when I started being anxious, I got away from everything and everyone and spent time with just me and God. I got plenty of rest. I went to bed each night in perfect peace. God said he would keep you in perfect peace whose mind was stayed on Him. Please believe me - you can cash that spiritual check of peace from God. It will not bounce!

I was ready now to face anything. I was fully equipped. The Word says, "The entrance of your word bringeth light." I knew God's Word was my light and I was walking in that light. I was living and breathing God's Words. The scripture says in Him we move, live and have our being. That scripture came alive. It was no longer information to me; it was now revelation.

There is a person in the Bible whose house was swept empty, and because God's Word was not living inside the person, the enemy was able to invade the house with more demons. I definitely was not that person. No, my house was full of God's promises, God's truth, and His ever-abiding love. My house was full of the assurance that whatever comes my way, I already had the victory. I knew my authority now. Even from a natural perspective knowledge is power. How much more powerful is spiritual knowledge? I was in spiritual power. Because I knew my spiritual power, the demonic force of fear did not have a chance - not when God is your protector. I was speaking and decreeing from a point of victory. I was using my Spiritual weaponry. I was using my Spiritual artillery. I was using my faith, for without it I knew I could not please God. I was no longer pleasing the enemy with my fear, but I was now pleasing our loving Father God with my Faith. I was saying, "Goodbye fear."

As I stated earlier, fear is nothing but a thief. I was no longer going to allow that thief called fear to come in and rule my life. It was barking up the wrong tree now. I not only had knowledge, but I also had understanding. I had my own armor now, standing from a position of victory. Join with me and take your rightful position.

I was not going to allow the enemy to steal this glorious peace that I was walking in. It was too precious. Trusting in God became my hope, my joy and my peace. You can get there too. The reason the process appears to be difficult is because we have believed those demonic lies for so long. But this is your day to release those fears and walk by faith.

Take a stand; go in the right direction by putting your foot on the accelerator towards faith and denounce those fears. Say, "`Victory is mine in the name of Jesus." Let those words come out of your mouth. Embrace those words. God is our life. Oh! I am so glad God walked with me through it and assured me victory was mine.

I would like you to know that I did not share my journey with everyone because that's how the Holy Spirit led me, so for those that share their personal journey during the process, I don't see anything wrong with that either. When God is speaking to you it is personal, and that's all I will say to that. I did later share my story with my eldest sister, who has since gone home to be with the Lord, and I believe it brought strength to her during times of struggles.

During that journey in my life, I continued to base myself in God's presence. I focused on only positive things. I refused to entertain anything that would take me out of a place of peace. I did not look at any disturbing news. I allowed God to create that safe place for me as I abided in His protection. I made my requests known to God. I asked God to lead me during that journey and provide me wisdom as to what to do. I relied on the Holy Spirit's guidance.

I made one request to God: no chemotherapy. I stood on one of my favorite scriptures Mark 11:24 which states, "Therefore I say unto you, what things soever ye desire, when ye pray, believe that ye receive them, and ye shall have them". I do encourage you that whatever you are believing God for, you need to be specific as to what you want and that's what I did. God answered my request. I realize that chemotherapy has been used to prevent the spread of disease, so I am not making an argument regarding that. The point I am making is that I made a request unto God and He answered my prayer. I went through surgery in peace and several weeks of radiation in peace. I continued to travel with my job in peace and the truth of the matter is, very few people knew what I was going through. I repeat I lived in peace.

I was still encouraging people during this time as well. I even became unmindful because I was resting so much in Jesus. I was carrying Jesus' burden and not mine. Fear had lost its power over me. Jesus was so faithful during the process with me. He did not allow me to be tempted above that I was able to handle. Today I am cancer-free, but most of all I am fear-free. Hallelujah!

The "heat" of faith-filled words

You may ask, "Has fear tried to tempt you since?" I say, yes but trying and succeeding are different. I have learned to resist the devil and he will flee. I know my authority now. I understand the power of my words and that I can use the Word of God over any circumstance. The enemy never can and never will be able to stand the "heat" of faith-filled words.

Many of you have heard the saying: "If you can't stand the heat, get out of the kitchen."

Well for me, I have learned that the way you resist the enemy is to give him the heat of God's Word. In my life now, I have been doing a lot of resisting from a position of victory and not defeat. See, I learned that my strength lies in God. I trust Him and Him alone, as He reminded me that I am never alone. God walked with me and showed me that He had me - and He did. Jesus is a faithful High Priest, and He truly is the great physician.

This peace that I have has made me realize that it is truly time to be about my Father's business. I want to see others healed, delivered and set free. I want to see others step into their destiny, their purpose. I want to see others take their stand and know the authority God has given them. I want to see others set free.

I believe despite my inner turmoil when I was battling with fear, even as a little girl I had an overwhelming compassion for others. I remember once when my big brother was being a little rebellious as a child. I was concerned about him. I was praying for him and God brought me such peace in a dream. In my dream, there was a war going on and I knew that my brother was on the wrong side. I somehow slipped over to the enemy line to get him to come with me. I don't remember much now regarding that dream, but what I do remember is that when I opened my eyes, he was on the right side. I will say to you, my readers, that the enemy has tormented you in the camp of fear long enough. I believe your eyes are opening up now, and you are coming out of the enemy's camp of fear. You are headed to the right side.

I encourage you to make declarations and stand on God's prom-ises. Every good and per-fect gift comes from God. It's time we become fear chasers. How

"THE ENEMY HAS TORMENTED YOU IN THE CAMP OF FEAR LONG ENOUGH"

do you chase fear? With the Word of God. Have you ever thought about why Jesus was led by the Spirit into the wilderness? I believe in order to show us that we can defeat any temptation that comes our way with the Word of God. How did Jesus overcome every temptation? With the Word of God. God's Word works. It is time we believe it, apply it, and live it. Say out loud, "God's Word works and His Word is working mightily in me." Aren't you ready to truly take God at His Word? That's freedom. Be free today.

I enjoy reading the story of David and Goliath. All of Israel were afraid to face the giant Goliath, yet David did not back down from Goliath. He told Saul that he will go and fight him.

David was not afraid. Why? Because he had already seen what God could and would do. He knew that if God had delivered him once, He would do it again. David was ready. It's time for you to be ready. That Goliath of fear has tormented you long enough. What did David do? He charged Goliath - but not on his own strength. Goliath came to David with a sword, and with a spear and with a shield, but David came to Goliath in the name of the Lord. He faced that Goliath but he did not face it alone.

Fear is nothing but a Goliath in your life, and you do not have to face it alone. You have already won the victory because the fight is fixed. Goliath had lost before he knew what hit him. A shepherd boy who believed and

> **"FEAR IS NOTHING BUT A GOLIATH IN YOUR LIFE AND YOU DO NOT HAVE TO FACE IT ALONE"**

trusted God saved Israel that day. David said in Psalm 23:" Ye though I walk through the valley of the shadow of death, I will fear no evil." That complete trust and dependency on God gave David and Israel the victory.

Let's look at another story in the Bible. I also like reading the book of Esther. Queen Esther, as she is referred to, had an opportunity to go before the king to save the people of Israel, but she was afraid initially. There was a great need for Esther (a Jew) to go before the king because a decree had been signed off by the king that every people (the Jews) who did not follow the king's laws would be destroyed. Esther's uncle (Mordecai) wanted her to go before the king on the people's behalf. Esther tried to explain that whosoever come into the king's court, male or female who was not called, by law would be put to death, unless the king extended the golden scepter to indicate that they may live. She noted that she had not been called by the king for 30 days. Mordecai, and I am paraphrasing, said to Esther, "You can't hold your peace; no, Esther you've got to face those fears." Esther knew what she had to do. Maybe she felt at first "backed against the wall" but she could not deny her purpose and the calling on her life. She asked the Jews to fast for three days with her as she agreed to go before the king, which was unlawful to do without an invitation. Esther came to the resolve, "If I perish, I perish." Wow! those words are powerful. Esther was ready to fulfill her ultimate calling, and fear was no longer in the way - even if it meant death. We know Esther did not perish when she went before the king, as God always protects us when we are obedient to His will. I want to encourage you that fear cannot seal your fate, because we serve the King of Kings and Lord of Lords. Amen!

See, Esther was raised for a purpose; we all have a purpose. We must also realize that our purpose is never about just us, but it is about God's plans for us. As a result of Esther listening to her uncle, she walked in obedience and the children of Israel were protected. What if Esther had allowed fear to keep her from doing what was right? What if she had succumbed to that inner turmoil? The outcome would have possibly been totally different. But Esther did not yield to fear and neither should you!

When fear dominates our lives, we can miss out on opportunities or even blessings all because we yielded to that demonic sprit called fear. Do you see it now? Do you see that we do not need to yield to fear because God always delivers us when we walk in our purpose? In fact, Isaiah 1:19 says, "If ye be willing and obedient, ye shall eat the good of the land:" God wants us to enjoy His manifold blessings.

Can I entertain you with one more story in the Bible? It's about Moses. God had chosen Moses to deliver the children of Israel out of Egypt, but Moses did not feel he was adequate. He too was afraid. He felt he had a speech problem. God asked him, "Who made man's mouth?" God never expects anything of you that he has not equipped you to do. I heard a minister say that He never sends you into a battle that you cannot win. God knew that He would have Moses' brother Aaron help. He knew Pharaoh would not want to let the children of Israel go, yet He knew His signs and wonders would eventually make a believer out of Pharaoh and that Pharaoh would finally let them go.

Maybe you have a fear of public speaking. It is time you realize you are an overcomer. I encourage you to step out there and speak. Let God use you. He can and wants to use you. We see God using an animal to talk in the Bible, so He can surely use you. God wants you to be confident in your ability that He has placed inside of you.

Psalm 27: 1 says, "The LORD is my light and my salvation; whom shall I fear? the LORD is the strength of my life; of whom shall I be afraid?"

I am ready to take this wisdom of No More Fear to my family, friends, and to the nations. Fear has crippled us long enough, but we are enlightened now and because we know this, it is time to go and do what God has called us to do.

THE BATTLE IS FIXED
FOR YOU TO WIN

These stories in the Bible and many others show the power and hand of God over our lives. They are constant reminders that each fight we encounter is from a point of victory and not defeat. How? Because the battle is already fixed for you to win. I pray I have encouraged you to close the door to fear. You have to know beyond a shadow of doubt that the peace of God is with you. You can face and walk through whatever the situation, whatever the fear, as I did with the strength of God. I walked through that very dark door of fear and I survived, and so will you.

"YOU ARE DESIGNED TO MAKE IT. YOU ARE DESIGNED TO SURVIVE"

You are designed to make it. You are designed to survive. God's grace is and will always be enough. Fear no longer had a hold on me, and I believe it will no longer have a hold on you. I was living in peace. My life had forever changed. I chased God's Word and God's Word chased me.

You ask: "Can that really happen to me?" I say yes because God loves us all. Just like he helped me, He will help you also. He wants you to live a life of peace more than you can ever know. He reminded me of that on that day I was driving home to share that disturbing news regarding my cancer prognosis. Psalm 51 tells us, "A broken heart and contrite spirit He will in no wise cast aside." It is yours for the asking, for the believing, for the receiving. Whatever your fear or inner turmoil is you can be free; take a stand today. Ask God to help you and He truly will; I am a living testimony.

My daughter and I wrote a declaration for our women's prayer group as it is a reminder to us who we are in Christ and that God has given us a voice to declare who we are using the Word of God, and I would like to share with you: We are mighty women of God. We are blessed and highly favored. No weapons formed against us or our households shall ever prosper. Our lives are saturated with God's love and peace. Our households are blessed. We lack nothing. We are prosperous healthy and whole. There are no feeble persons in our households. We have more than enough. We are lenders and not borrowers. We are the head and not the tail. We are from above and not beneath. For God has brought us to the palace for such a time as this. For this is our Declaration.

At the end of this book, the final instruction page encourages you to write a declaration confessing your deliverance from fear.

I invite you to say this prayer:

Dear Lord,

I take you at your Word that you have not given me a spirit of fear, but of power, love, and a sound mind. Deliver me from my fears as I put my trust in you. God, from this day forward, I cast all my cares on you as you have promised to never leave me or forsake me. From this day forward I stand on your Word: No More Fear.

SUMMARY

Below is a summary of steps I recommend if you are battling with fear. These recommendations are what got me to the place of refusing to fear. I believe they will help you as well. Please know that your ultimate deliverance will start with believing and applying the Word of God to your life. You must make God's Word personal to you and to your situation. God's Word is the ultimate weapon that will bring healing and deliverance to you. His Word is our medicine. I heard someone say that God's medicine does not have

> "GOD'S WORD IS OUR LIVING BREAD THAT WE MUST PARTAKE OF EVERYDAY...RENEW YOUR MIND WITH THE WORD OF GOD"

any bad side effects. Hallelujah! I know all will agree that's the best type of medicine to take.

God's Word is our living bread that we must partake of every day. Yes, God's Word brings life to us. It revitalizes us. Renew your mind with the Word of God. Maybe some of you are Christians who just need to reconnect back closer to God. Go ahead and reconnect. Let God's Word be a lamp unto your feet and a light unto your path. Reconnecting to God will be the best decision you can ever make. Remember, if

God is in the ring of life with you, everything is predestined to work out. You are destined to win because the Lord of Host is with you.

Summary of Steps When Battling with Fear:

- First, realize fear is not just an emotion, but an evil force trying to torment you.
- Acknowledge the fear and inner turmoil before God
- If there are several types of fears, release them to God
- Make your request known to God and ask God to heal you and set you free
- Repent that you have been more fearful of Satan than trusting God
- Replace fear with faith by reading and meditating on the Word of God
- Find specific scriptures regarding your situation in the Word of God
- Surround yourself with believers who are really praying for you
- Refuse to entertain doubt and worry, even if this means shutting your mind off
- Seek the Wisdom of God in your situation and be obedient to what He says

- Pray for others who are battling fear or dealing with a similar situation, if you are aware of them
- Make declarations that you are delivered from fear

These are not all-inclusive, but I pray God will speak to you and give you wisdom. I believe you can take these same principles and deal with anything the enemy may be trying to do in your life. Remember - Satan is all bark.

Recommended scriptures to read every day:

Philippians 4:6-7: Be careful for nothing; but in everything with prayer and supplication with thanksgiving let your requests be made known to God. And the peace of God which passeth all understanding, shall keep your hearts and minds through Christ Jesus.

Psalm 34:4-5: I sought the Lord, and he heard me, and delivered me from all my fears.

Psalm 56:3: What time I am afraid, I will trust in thee.

2 Timothy 1:7: For God hath not given us the spirit of fear; but of power, and of love, and of a sound mind.

1 Peter 5:6-7: Humble yourselves therefore under the mighty hand of God, that he may exalt you in due time. Casting all your care upon him; for He careth for you.

1 John 4:18: There is no fear in love; but perfect love casteth out fear: because fear hath torment. He that feareth is not made perfect in love.

You are now at the final step in the book. Now it is time to complete the Instructions Worksheet.

Maybe this is the most important step of all. If you are at this point, then you have read the entire book. You now know the answer to the three important points discussed in the book:

What is Fear?

What is the Root of Fear?

How to Get Rid of Fear?

I praise God that you are here. You are now knowledgeable, as you know your power and your authority. Your deliverance will now come from a personal journey with God. I have shared my journey and I have been transparent and even vulnerable at times, but now it is up to you. You possess all the tools and knowledge to now be free. If my transparency gets you to the point of no more fear, then it is truly worth it.

Final Step: Instruction Worksheet:

Get your Bible out - it is time to use your weapon!

First: List specific scriptures regarding your deliverance (as many as you are led to) – make it personal:

1.

2.

3.

I encourage you to say those scriptures out loud and meditate on them day and night. Say them until you get a release in your spirit, where your mind is saturated with the Word of God and closed to the deception and lies of Satan.

God said to Joshua: "This book of the law shall not depart out of your mouth; but thou shalt meditate therein day and night, that thou mayest observe to do according to all that is written therein: for then thou shalt make thy way prosperous, and then thou shalt have good success." (Joshua 1:8).

Lastly: Create your personal declaration regarding your deliverance from fear to recite every day:

I Declare...

1._____

_____

_____

_____

_____

2._____

_____

_____

_____

_____

3._____

_____

_____

_____

4._____

_____

_____

_____

5._____

_____

_____

_____

Dear Heavenly Father,

I have been transparent and shared my own personal struggles that occurred throughout my life regarding fear to the readers of this book. I pray that they see through my own personal journey that they are not alone. Whatever fear that they are dealing with, God, I pray that you set them free as you set me free. Lord, open their eyes that they may see that fear no longer has to dominate their lives. You are such a loving Father who wants us to put our complete trust in you. I won't say that I learned this too late, but later than I wish I had. Lord, please let each reader know that just like the fear came, it can be gone when they put all their trust in you. That's what happened to me, and I believe it will happen to them also. Lord, I believe you have heard my prayer and from this day forward, I stand with the readers of this book that they are now free from fear. In the mighty name of Jesus, I pray. Amen.

I celebrate with you as you have to come to the place: Goodbye Fear!

Lightning Source UK Ltd.
Milton Keynes UK
UKHW020627250422
402014UK00007B/167